LOST
WATFORD

JOHN COOPER

AMBERLEY

Also by John Cooper

A Harpenden Childhood Remembered: Growing up in the 1940s and '50s
Making Ends Meet: A Working Life Remembered
A Postcard From Harpenden: A Nostalgic Glimpse of the Village Then and Now
Watford Through Time
A Postcard From Watford
Harpenden Through Time
Rickmansworth, Croxley Green & Chorleywood Through Time
Hertfordshire's Historic Inland Waterway: Batchworth to Berkhamsted
Harpenden: The Postcard Collection
Watford History Tour
Harpenden: A Village in Wartime
Harpenden History Tour

To my darling wife Bet and all the family

First published 2020

Amberley Publishing
The Hill, Stroud
Gloucestershire, GL5 4EP

www.amberley-books.com

British Library Cataloguing in Publication Data.

A catalogue record for this book is available from the British Library.

ISBN 978 1 4456 9279 1 (print)
ISBN 978 1 4456 9280 7 (ebook)

Origination by Amberley Publishing.
Printed in the UK.

Contents

Introduction 4

1 The Pond and The Parade 7

2 In and Around the High Street 17

3 St Albans Road to Garston 37

4 Watford Junction to Leavesden 47

5 Cassio Hamlet to Hunton Bridge 58

6 Rickmansworth Road and West Watford 66

7 Along the Canal to Cassiobury 75

8 Entertainment and Leisure 87

Acknowledgements 96

Introduction

Through the superb black and white and colour images contained on the following pages of *Lost Watford*, the reader is taken on a fascinating journey of discovery to find what has disappeared from our town forever and been consigned to memory, or has radically changed to what it was originally.

Standing on the steps of the dominant Town Hall building today, the centre of local civic administration, watching the rush-hour traffic streaming relentlessly down the underpass or heading towards the roundabout, it is difficult to imagine that over a hundred years ago this was a peaceful area known as the Four Crossroads. In those days, all that existed was a signpost indicating the directions to the High Street, St Albans Road, Hempstead Road and Rickmansworth Road, the only traffic being the horse-drawn haywains going to market.

A short distance from the Crossroads was – and still is, although much changed – the pond, a picturesque oasis where in the early days of the twentieth century, carters used to water their horses in the heat of a summer's afternoon, or where excited youngsters would sail a toy yacht. Today, with the area pedestrianised and a footbridge traversing the water, it now provides a quiet haven to sit and while away a few leisurely moments.

One of the more unpopular losses to the town was that of the historic, castellated, Tudor-style Cassiobury Park gates in Rickmansworth Road, which were originally built as the entrance to the long driveway leading to Cassiobury House. It was on Friday 24 July 1970 when the demolition men started to reduce part of Watford's heritage to rubble in order to facilitate an essential road widening scheme, an act that was deeply felt by Watfordians.

Cassiobury House itself, once the seat of the Earls of Essex, had suffered a similar fate forty-three years earlier when following the death of the 7th Earl in 1916, his wife Adele, the countess dowager who had sold the estate in 1922 for building development, was unable to find a purchaser for the house, which was then left empty and derelict for a further five years until the magnificent building was razed to the ground. The lasting legacy is the beautiful award-winning Cassiobury Park, once part of the Essex estate and now the jewel in Watford's crown.

Many readers will fondly remember Watford's two premier department stores: Clements on The Parade and Cawdell's further down the High Street. These emporiums, both well established in the town, sold all types of goods for every occasion and were indeed a shopper's paradise where, on entering, one was greeted by an immaculately dressed and debonair floor walker complete with a red carnation buttonhole – a sign of the good old-fashioned service, courtesy and personal attention that have now passed into the mists of time. Cawdell's was the first to go when a decision to build Charter Place was made, while Clements eventually closed its doors in 2004 after trading for 106 years. Today the old Victorian building is occupied by a B&M retail outlet.

Gone too is the old Watford open-air market, where on a Tuesday the weekly livestock sales were held, attracting farmers and traders from miles around – a smelly and noisy place in which to venture. With the gradual decline of brewing in the town, the end finally came when Allied

Breweries, previously Benskins, ceased production in the early 1970s – the end of an era and a great loss to Watford. Although the site in Lower High Street was gradually demolished and redeveloped in 1979, the fine Georgian house that had once belonged to John Dyson, the owner of the Cannon Brewery later purchased by Joseph Benskin, remains today as Watford's prestigious museum.

Probably a good example of a loss turning into a massive gain would be at Leavesden, where during the Second World War, as an aerodrome and aircraft factory, a large number of Mosquitoe and Halifax aeroplanes were produced. The site eventually became a subsidiary of Rolls-Royce, building helicopter engines until closure in 1992. During the new millennium, just like the proverbial 'phoenix rising from the ashes', Leavesden took on a new lease of life when Warner Bros acquired the site to become one of the largest film-making studios in the world.

Possibly the most favourite form of entertainment during the interwar years of the 1920s and '30s and the Second World War was the cinema, in what was generally considered it's 'golden age' and, in this sphere, Watford was well catered for. Cinemas such as the Odeon and Gaumont on The Parade, the Carlton in Clarendon Road, the Essoldo in King Street and the Odeon in St Albans Road to name but a few, where for a couple of hours, patrons could forget the realities of everyday life and enjoy the latest feature films in the smoky atmosphere of the auditorium. Sadly, though, these movie theatres with their art deco façades and garish neon lighting are now but a memory, as one by one the final curtain came down and the doors closed for the last time.

Despite the many losses, changes and modernisation that have taken place in and around the town as part of continuing progress, Watford can be justifiably proud of its history and can continue to treasure all that it still has for the benefit of future generations.

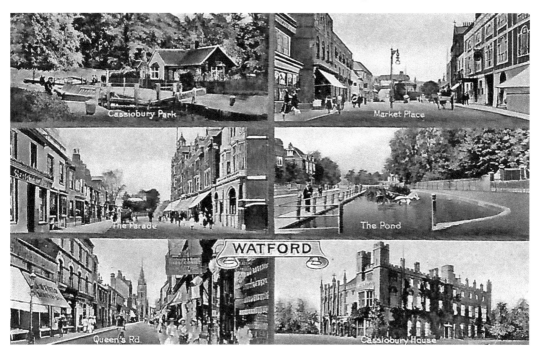

Memories of bygone Watford.

Arthur New, butcher of Vicarage Road.

The Pond area with the Odeon cinema.

Section 1

The Pond and The Parade

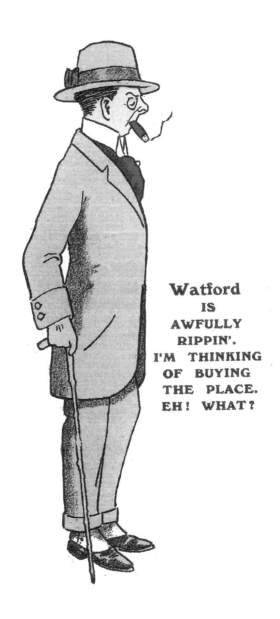

The Crossroads

The old snapshot above, taken during the late 1890s or early 1900s, shows a wintry scene at the Crossroads, the junction at the northern end of the town where Hempstead, Rickmansworth and St Albans Roads met with the High Street. Up until the mid-1930s, control of converging traffic at this point had been carried out by an AA patrolman, but with the ever-growing volume of cars and other vehicles this task was becoming increasingly difficult, and the decision was made to build a roundabout. The building in the background is The Elms, an early eighteenth-century mansion that was later demolished in preparation for the construction of the new Town Hall, which was officially opened on 5 January 1940.

The Town Hall Roundabout

With the steady increase in the volume of traffic, a major reconstruction programme commenced in 1936 to transform the Crossroads into a roundabout. Unlike now, vehicles could travel up and down the High Street, which then formed the main route to Bushey, Harrow and London. With traffic congestion becoming ever more acute in and around the town centre, work began in 1972 on building the new St Albans Road underpass, a far cry from the earlier idyllic images taken so long ago. In the background can be seen the splendid new Town Hall and municipal offices that were constructed on the site of The Elms, originally known as Town End House, an early eighteenth-century mansion that had occupied a position on one corner of the Crossroads.

The Pond

Photographed countless times and the subject of numerous picture postcards, the pond situated on The Parade at the northern end of the High Street has provided a constant source of pleasure and delight to thousands of people for well over a hundred years. Although not 'lost' in the true sense of the word, this picturesque oasis in Watford's town centre has seen many changes, from excited youngsters floating their toy yachts in the early 1900s and horses being watered in the heat of a summer's afternoon, to the peaceful scene of today as office workers snatch a few brief moments enjoying a lunchtime snack on a bench by the water's edge. By the early 1950s, with railings now in place all round and traffic freely passing up and down the High Street, the days of watering horses was long gone. Today, with the area now pedestrianised, the pond is a quiet haven where one can while away a few leisurely moments.

The Odeon Cinema

Situated on The Parade adjacent to the picturesque Watford Pond is the majestic-looking Odeon cinema with its distinctive prominent dome above the main entrance. The performance depicted in the postcard is the 1954 film *Suddenly*, starring Frank Sinatra. Originally built as the Plaza in 1929 with a seating capacity of 2,060, it was at the time the largest cinema auditorium in Hertfordshire. In July 1936 the Odeon circuit acquired the Plaza, the change of name coming into effect on Monday 12 October, providing 1,253 seats in the stalls and 736 in the balcony. The Odeon eventually closed its doors on Saturday 30 November 1963 and was demolished in February 1964.

The Odeon Cinema

The above picture shows the interior of the Odeon in November 1939 where the screening of an early propaganda film, *The Lion Has Wings*, was about to be shown to the Mayor of Watford, Alderman Lewin Halsey Andrews. The film depicted 'a mass raid by Luftwaffe bombers turning back in fear and confusion at the sight of Britain's terrifying balloon barrage'.

The Parade

With the loss of the Odeon in 1963, the site was redeveloped into a new building housing one of Watford's early nightclubs, Top Rank Watford Suite, with Caters supermarket occupying the ground floor. This part of the town, as seen in these two images of the late 1960s/early 1970s, depicts many long-gone shops such as Bailey's, the radio and television dealers, Swann's leather and fancy goods, and Peter Spivey sports outfitters. A favourite meeting place in those days was the Cookery Nook, since closed, a quintessentially English tearoom with a Tudor beam ceiling, where delicious scones and light lunches were on offer.

Monmouth House

This early seventeenth-century, Grade II listed building was constructed by Sir Robert Carey, 1st Earl of Monmouth, who in 1603 took the news of Queen Elizabeth's death to her successor, King James I. Following Robert's own death, the house was occupied as a dower house by his widow Elizabeth until her demise in 1641. In 1771 the accommodation was divided into two and altered in 1830, with the north part being called Monmouth House and the south The Platts. During the late 1920s, the building was converted to business premises and retail outlets, retaining the name of Monmouth House.

The Fire Station

In the summer of 1900, the new Watford fire station with its unique-looking frontage was opened next to the Urban District Council offices in the High Street where Gade House is now situated. To celebrate the occasion, an informal celebratory dinner was held on the premises for forty people, which included members of the Town Brigade, Croxley Mills Brigade and the Sedgwick Brigade, the latter having been formed in 1876 when Mr F. Sedgwick obtained a horse-drawn Shand and Mason steam-operated fire engine, popularly known as a 'steamer', for his brewery. Although the Sedgwick Brewery Brigade was an independent fire service, they very often assisted the Town Brigade at major fires. The fire station remained in the High Street until 1961, when they moved to their newly built £80,000 premises at the junction of Rickmansworth and Whippendell Roads, operating from there for a further forty-eight years until a new £5 million state-of-the-art station opened in Lower High Street on 19 November 2009.

High Street

The above image from the early 1960s shows the changing face of this part of the High Street, with Upton House, previously the centre of local government, already flattened and the fire station awaiting demolition.

14

Clements

It was a sad day for Watford when Clements, once the town's premier department store, finally closed its doors in January 2004 after trading for 106 years from the same Victorian building. Opening in 1898, Clements sold all types of goods for every occasion and was seen as the inspiration for the TV comedy series *Are You Being Served?* On entering what was indeed a shopper's paradise, one was greeted by an immaculately dressed and debonair floor walker complete with a red carnation buttonhole. Although the lovely building remains, it just does not seem the same without the shopping emporium that was Clements.

Clements

Another view of Clements department store, this time taken in the 1950s. Also seen is a sign advertising the location of the Brass Lantern, a tearoom and small restaurant that occupied the first floor of this fifteenth-century timbered building, where light lunches and dinners were once served. Like so many similar establishments from those bygone days, the Brass Lantern has long since disappeared.

The Parade, South of the Flyover

These two lovely coloured images of the Parade south of the flyover, depicted in the centre of the top picture, show the area, now pedestrianised, starting to take on the appearance of how it looks today. Although shopfronts such as Clements, the Kardomah coffee shop and Copperfields restaurant, together with much of the street furniture, planters and advertising hoardings, have now all gone, these have now been replaced by different retail outlets and more updated seating and features.

Section 2

In and Around the High Street

I am enjoying the best of good Spirits at WATFORD.

Declaration of the Poll

A large expectant crowd had gathered outside the Corn Exchange next to the Essex Arms Hotel in the High Street on the cold wintry day of 24 January 1906 to hear the declaration of the poll between the Liberal candidate, Nathaniel Micklem, and the Conservative, the Right Honourable T. F. Halsey. The result was a win for the Liberal candidate, who defeated the Conservative by a majority of 1,476. The message on the above postcard, sent on 22 January, refers to a large Liberal meeting that had been held nine days prior to the poll in the old Clarendon Hall on 15 January: 'Great L. (Liberal) meeting tonight – procession from L. Club headed by brass band & all sorts. I hear they are going to appeal against C. (Conservative) member at St Albans on ground of unfair play.' Over 110 years later, with the buildings long since gone, the area has now been engulfed into the Intu Watford shopping centre extension.

High Street – Clarendon Road to Market Street

A nostalgic glimpse of the town centre taken during the interwar years of the 1920s, where the pavements are filled with busy shoppers thronging the well-known High Street shops such as Saxone Shoes, W. H. Smith & Son, Dudley's the costumiers and James Walker the jewellers, where among other exquisite items on offer, a Rolex precision watch can be purchased and repairs undertaken at moderate charges. With the fascinating detail depicted in the above image of an age long since passed, much of the charm and atmosphere from those bygone days has sadly been lost forever.

High Street

Captured on a warm, sunny summer's day in the 1970s, this picture of virtually the same view as the image above shows the various transformations that have taken place within the intervening years, with the inevitable changes in shop names, the introduction of yellow lines and the resulting lack of traffic. Establishments such as the popular local restaurant and caterers Buck's, founded in 1868 by Mr and Mrs Philip Buck, and W. Wren & Sons who sold bags, trunks and quality sports and leather goods are now just memories of a past age. Today, with the ceaseless march of progress, the view on the right-hand side has undergone a dramatic metamorphosis with the opening of the new Intu Watford shopping centre extension in 2018.

Market Day

Another busy Tuesday in the High Street is depicted in this circa 1910 image as the weekly livestock market gets under way, a market that was granted by charter in the reign of Henry I (1100–35). Although attracting farmers and traders alike from miles around, the High Street was a smelly and noisy place in which to venture, and for many the general merchandise market held on a Saturday must have been far more appealing. Trading remained in the High Street until 1928 when stallholders were transferred to a new site in Red Lion Yard, while the cattle market transferred to Stones Alley, just behind the post office in Market Street, where it remained until its ultimate closure in the last week of December 1959. To the right of the picture above can just be seen the premises of the well-known drapers and furnishing store of Cawdell's, since demolished as part of the Central Car Park redevelopment scheme in the mid-1970s.

Saturday Market

Following the market's move from the High Street to Red Lion Yard in 1928, trading was initially carried out in the open, although it was eventually covered over four years later. In the mid-1970s, the bustling Corporation Market, seen below in 1950, transferred to a new location in Charter Place where on a Tuesday, Friday and Saturday a variety of high-class goods and services were on offer to the stallholders' many loyal customers. During the drab, austere post-war years following the cessation of hostilities in 1945, rationing was still very much in evidence, although with clothes being derationed in 1949, there appears to be quite a keen interest in the stall selling babywear, frocks, wool sets and socks. Today, the market is located in what was once the car park for Clements department store.

High Street – the Old Market Place

Two coloured snapshots from the 1950s where once the hustle and bustle of a busy livestock market took place. In 1905, James Cawdell opened his drapery and furnishings shop at No. 71 High Street next to the Essex Arms, which he later purchased in 1929. During the early 1930s both buildings were demolished, with the site being redeveloped into the white art deco edifice featured on the right of the picture. The clock was added at a later date. Cawdell's proved to be a very popular department store to their many loyal customers and was second only to Clements further along the High Street. In 1973 time was called on trading, and the building was demolished to make way for the entrance to the new Charter Place development, subsequently completely revamped as part of the 2018 Intu Watford shopping centre extension.

The Compasses Public House

The Compasses public house, situated on the corner of the High Street and Market Street, pictured above circa 1890, was built around 1725. In 1888/9, following a partial demolition of the premises next door when Market Street was opened up, a fifteenth-century window was discovered, which is still preserved to this day. The legend on the accompanying plaque states: 'The above window was removed from the old Compasses Inn demolished in 1928. It is believed to have been one of the windows of the Rest House which stood on this site in the fifteenth century to serve those attending Watford Market. It is noteworthy that Watford Market received its Charter in the reign of Henry I.'

Church Street

With the beautiful Church of St Mary (one of the largest churches in Hertfordshire) as a backdrop, the view in both pictures shows several buildings on the left-hand side, opposite the church. These were the National School, the parish workhouse erected in 1721, and a small fire appliance shed, now all gone to be replaced by a multistorey car park. Further up Church Street is New Street and the infamous Ballard's Buildings, while in the distance on the High Street is the historic One Bell public house, now boarded up, it's future uncertain.

THE PARISH CHURCH, WATFORD.

New Street and Ballard's Buildings

This picture of a squalid, rundown area of Watford taken circa 1914 depicts New Street, a narrow road that ran from the Market Place to Church Street. The courtyard entrance to Ballard's Buildings is just out of camera shot on the right of the image where lived a motley assortment of residents, including a rat catcher who no doubt made a reasonable living from his somewhat unenviable trade. Originally intended as temporary dwellings to accommodate a large number of railway workers in the 1830s, the poor housing lasted for almost a hundred years until they were demolished under a slum clearance order in 1926. Today, where once the unsavoury and dilapidated buildings used to be, a multistorey car park now stands, dominated by the imposing structure of St Mary's Parish Church.

PARISH CHURCHYARD, WATFORD, SHOWING FIG TREE GROWING OUT OF TOMB

The Fig Tree Tomb

One of Watford's strangest legends is that of the Fig Tree Tomb in St Mary's Churchyard. So the myth goes, a lady who was an atheist was buried in a vault close to the wall of the church. On her deathbed she is reported to have expressed a wish that if there was a God a fig tree might grow from her heart. Whatever the story, a fig tree did indeed grow from the tomb and remained there until it died in the severe winter of 1962/3. The fig tree can just be seen to the left of the large window on the right-hand side of the early 1900s picture above. However, another version of the legend states that the unbeliever was a man, one Ben Wangford, who lived in the mid-1800s and was also buried in the churchyard. The tomb remains although the inscription is unreadable due to erosion, which may account for some of the mystery surrounding this intriguing tale.

FIG TREE GROWING OUT OF A TOMB, WATFORD.

The Free School

Built in 1704, the Free School was founded by Elizabeth Fuller as a charity 'for the teaching of forty poor boys and fourteen poor girls of Watford in good literature and manners'. With the help of endowments and bequests, the institution survived for almost 180 years when charity schools as such ceased to function. Following its closure in 1882, the establishment was transferred to a new building in Derby Road called the Endowed School, the precursor of the Watford Grammar Schools for Boys and Girls. This elegant Grade II listed Queen Anne building is now privately owned by Recovery In-Sight Social Enterprise (RISE), a charity providing advice, training and well-being for people affected by mental health difficulties.

Essex Almshouses

These beautifully preserved Grade II listed almshouses in Church Street were built in 1580 by Francis Russell, 2nd Duke of Bedford, so that 'eight poor women might inhabit and be maintained in the said eight almshouses'. Due to their dilapidated condition in the early 1930s, a successful appeal was made to preserve the buildings, which today remain the oldest inhabited dwellings in Watford. For safety reasons, access to the almshouses is now from the gardens to the rear, with the front doors onto Church Street being permanently closed as 'false' doors.

27

High Street – Junction with Queen's Road

A bright sunny day is depicted in this unused postcard above showing the junction of Queen's Road with the High Street in the early 1950s. King Street is just down on the right-hand side past Woolworths, and where Mrs L. Packer was 'mine host' of the King's Arms public house on the corner of what was once the gate lodge of the carriageway leading to Watford Place. A McDonald's fast-food outlet now occupies the site of the old inn. On the opposite side of the High Street, where Boots the Chemists once traded, is now the imposing entrance to the Intu Watford shopping centre, which opened its doors in 1992 as the Harlequin Centre. Boots is now one of the stores within the complex.

King Street

Taken from King Street in April 1990, the above photo shows the construction of the main entrance to the Harlequin, now the Intu Watford shopping centre in the High Street, and the back of the new Woolworths site, now occupied by McDonald's. With redevelopment continuing along Queen's Road opposite, it won't be long before the large distinctive building, the old Westminster Bank in the background, is reduced to rubble as well. As with many other parts of the town, King Street has seen massive change: once extending as far as Lady's Close where the Girls' Grammar School is situated, before the introduction of the one-way system that bisected the road just past Watford Place. From 1889 until 1940, a police station occupied the site on the corner of Smith Street, but in 1961 a new public house, the aptly named Robert Peel (since closed), opened its doors on the same location where once drunks and vagabonds had been held in custody.

Queen Road, Watford

Queen's Road

These two charming picture postcards of the early 1900s depict a more tranquil way of life that has long since disappeared. Before the twentieth century ended, Queen's Road, one of Watford's busy shopping thoroughfares, was completely transformed as large swathes of the area were reduced to rubble following extensive demolition to make way for what was originally known as the Mars 1 project, better known as the new Harlequin shopping centre, now Intu Watford, which was completed in 1992. During the autumn of 1988, many private houses and retail premises, together with Clifford Street, Carey Place, Charles Street and Albert Street, were all lost as the bulldozers set to work on the 12-acre site.

QUEEN'S ROAD WATFORD

Maternity Home

Watford Maternity Home, straddling what is now the ring road, was opened at No. 21 King Street in 1935 and rebuilt in 1937 by the county council, who had taken over the management of the building from the County Nursing Home Association. Following a brief period as the Maternity Wing of the newly formed Watford General Hospital, it eventually closed in 1969 when a new maternity unit opened at the hospital in Vicarage Road. The home was demolished as part of a road-widening scheme, with new housing in King's Close now occupying part of the old site.

District Hospital

Built in 1885, the Cottage Hospital, later called the District Hospital, in Vicarage Road originally had nine beds at the time of its opening, but in 1897 a new six-bed ward and an operating theatre were added to mark the Diamond Jubilee of Queen Victoria. In 1903, new dining rooms and staff accommodation together with two additional six-bed wards were built to provide a total capacity of twenty-seven much needed beds. The inscription on a tablet at the front of the hospital states: 'This stone was laid by the Countess of Clarendon Nov. 4th. 1885'. Today, this old building is used for office accommodation.

High Street – Junction with King Street and Queen's Road

Frozen in time at midday, this lovely old 1920s photograph, taken just down from the junction with King Street and Queen's Road, shows the High Street looking north. The delightful shop frontages include the reputable premises of Benjamin Morse, the high-class jeweller and watchmaker situated next door to the motoring business of Messrs Tucker Brothers, an authorised dealer for Morris Cars. On the opposite side of the road the well-known bazaar of Marks & Spencer can be seen, adjacent to Sketchley Dye Works and Boots the Chemists on the corner of Queen's Road. This truly superb image captures a slower and more genteel way of life in the early part of the twentieth century, now sadly lost to modernisation in the relentless march of progress.

High Street – Junction with King Street and Queen's Road

A similar view to the above image but taken fifty years later, in the 1970s. As to be expected, shopfront names such as Peter Adams, house furnishers, Curry's, television retailers and Swan's, furriers, have all gone, with obvious changes to the type of vehicles and pedestrians' clothing when compared to the earlier picture. Note too the introduction of the prohibitive yellow lines.

31

Woolworths

With the stark Woolworths store edifice above dominating the junction of the High Street with King Street in the early 1980s, the 'writing was already on the wall' for this popular local retailer, which eventually closed on 20 January 1990 to be replaced by a new building that housed, amongst others, a new McDonald's fast-food outlet. Many readers will fondly remember those days in the 1950s when the Woolworths store was set out with long counters on either side and one in the middle, with a gap so that customers could pass from one aisle to the other. Although the 'Nothing over 6d' motto had been abandoned during the first year of the Second World War, a favourite with the emerging teenager was the section that sold Embassy 78 rpm records, which were always that much cheaper than elsewhere. It was not until 2000 that another Woolworths opened near Clarendon Road, but the time was fast approaching when the High Street retail chain could no longer be sustained, with ultimate closure taking place in 2009 – the end of an era, and the loss of a much-loved shopping icon.

Lower High Street

To the extreme left of the picture just out of camera shot is Sedgwick's Brewery who, in 1876, obtained the first steam fire engine to be used in Watford. The appliance was owned by the brewery and attended most of the fires in the town at that time. Next door to the premises of Stagg Brothers at No. 229, and the butcher's shop of George Dumbelton is the Brewers Arms at No. 233, which was demolished in 1911. Another public house, the Leather Sellers Arms, is at No. 235 although a footpath between the buildings separates the two licensed premises. The licensee during the early 1930s was Thomas George Apps and the pub was demolished in 1960. Today, with widespread redevelopment having taken place in the area, Lower High Street has changed out of all recognition.

Benskin's Brewery

Following the death of John Dyson in 1867, the Cannon Brewery in Lower High Street was auctioned off and purchased by retired London hotelier Joseph Benskin and his partner, William Edmund Bradley, for £34,000. When Bradley left the partnership in 1870, Benskin continued with the business until his death seven years later. Over the years, Benskins gradually acquired all of the other Watford Breweries including Healey's in 1898, Sedgwick's in 1923 and Wells' in 1951. With a successful takeover bid from Ind Coope in 1957 together with further subsequent mergers, the company then became Allied Breweries continuing in Watford until production ceased in the early 1970s. Although the site was gradually demolished and redeveloped in 1979, the fine Georgian mansion that John Dyson's father, also John, had purchased in 1812 remains today as Watford's prestigious museum. The above picture shows Benskin's Brewery in 1949.

Benskin's Brewery

A single-horse van, probably dating from the turn of the nineteenth century, which won first prize at the Watford Carnival in 1936.

Watford Museum

A night-time view of the brewery offices in Lower High Street decorated and illuminated to celebrate the Silver Jubilee of George V on 6 May 1935, with the mansion now home to Watford Museum (below).

The Floods of 1903

The photographers of the day were indeed kept busy on Tuesday 16 June 1903, covering the floods that had devastated various parts of Watford – no mean feat under these abnormal conditions when one considers that they had to trundle around their heavy equipment, including possibly the new Sanderson plate camera and tripod. The enterprising delivery man above in Lower High Street appears to have solved the problem of loading and unloading his cart before departing on his rounds. Today, following a steady programme of redevelopment over the years, the area is completely unrecognisable to what it used to be over a century ago.

The Angel

Local photographer William Coles of Queen's Road captured this watery thoroughfare at the bottom of Lower High Street near the Angel public house following the flood of Tuesday 16 June 1903. This being market day, the two drovers can be seen leading a bull to the livestock sales in the centre of town. The Angel, which was built circa 1750, had only a short time left before it was demolished later in 1903. The approximate site is now occupied by George Ausden, scrap iron and metal merchant.

Bus Garage Depot

Due to the rapid growth of bus service provision at the Leavesden Road garage, much larger premises (coded WA) were provided in Lower High Street in 1925 under the management of the National Company. The garage was used by the London General Country Service from 1926, and subsequently operated by the London Transport Passenger Board. The two pictures show the main entrance to the depot and women cleaners hosing down one of the buses. Space was rented on the gas works site on the opposite side of the High Street next to the scrap metal business of George Ausden to accommodate those buses that were under repair, as can be seen on the inset image which also shows a group of the local Home Guard circa mid-1940. The bus garage closed in 1959 following the construction of a new depot in Garston. The High Street site is now a car park for retail stores such as B&Q.

Section 3
St Albans Road to Garston

St Albans Road – Junction with Station Road and Langley Road

Like many major crossroads in Watford, such as the junction of Langley and Station Roads with St Albans Road, considerable change has taken place since the early 1900s, the most obvious being the implementation of a road-widening scheme that resulted in the demolition of the buildings on the right-hand side. Part of the new dual carriageway was constructed from Station Road in late 1961 and the railway bridge was rebuilt in 1962/63. Although the shopfronts to the structures on the left have altered several times over the years, some of the original architecture still remains from first floor to roof level.

38

North-Western Clothing Stores

In the 1930s, the North-Western Clothing Stores at No. 158 St Albans Road proudly boasted a Bespoke Department where 'Clothing to Measure' was cut by 'experienced cutters and made by practical workmen' with 'all the most fashionable cloths for the present season'. Suits could be purchased from 21s 6d to 75s. For the less discerning, their Ready-made Department could cater for the needs of 'workmen's, engineers' and butchers' clothing'. In addition, the extensive selection of goods on offer included items ranging from calicoes, sheeting and linoleum to umbrellas, hosiery and collar studs – a mini emporium. A newsagent now occupies the premises and, although the stock may be different, still provides the same comprehensive and valuable service to the local community that was on offer by Mr Gale over eighty years earlier.

Watford Cash Bakers

A long-forgotten image taken in the halcyon days before the popularity of the car, where the horse and cart belonging to Watford Cash Bakers of No. 226 St Albans Road is waiting to set off on its deliveries, as seen in this rare Edwardian card posted to a Mrs Huggett of Snodland, Kent, on 26 March 1907. The message from Allan reads: 'No time for writing this week, will write next. We are up to our eyes in work. What do you think of this Billie Boy on the van?' No doubt the youngster was eagerly looking forward to what was probably his first trip out on the round.

St Albans Road – Junction with Station Road and Langley Road

This nostalgic snapshot taken in the early part of the twentieth century depicts a fairly busy St Albans Road, taken from the bridge looking towards the junction with Station Road and Langley Road. While the buildings on the left have long been demolished to make way for road widening, some of the architecture on the right has survived with little change to the first-floor level and above over the intervening years. Although it is virtually impossible to determine many of the shopfront names, some of the traders included a dispensing chemist, a corn and coal merchant, a perambulator manufacturer and a bootmaker, 'where repairs were neatly executed'.

St Albans Road – Junction with Cromer Road

This superb picture postcard from the summer of 1915 shows a St Albans Road, frozen in time, at the junction with Cromer Road, although today there is now no longer any access onto the main thoroughfare. On the right-hand side, the shop on the corner that undertakes piano repairs has what appears to be a selection of sheet music on display, while the window to the side of the entrance door is advertising the sale of 'Picture Post Cards' with a wide selection of 'Watford Views' available. Further down the road, an ironmonger's wares of washing baskets and a besom of twigs have spilled out onto the pavement, together with a sturdy-looking trelliswork arch and some rolls of wire netting. The turning on the right by the pillar box is Balmoral Road.

Leavesden Road

What a tremendous transition between these two images of Leavesden Road, with the top postcard dated 16 July 1909 featuring a rural country lane and the bottom photo showing the rapid development that has taken place in the intervening years. The small tobacconists and general store on the corner of Lowestoft Road, seen below, advertising Van Houten's and Rowntree's cocoa, Capstan cigarettes and Monsters Marvellous Minerals, 'Unequalled in Quality, Quantity and Price' has long since disappeared, as well as the delightful old gas lamp post on the kerb side. Apart from the obvious cosmetic changes, the vista today of this quiet-looking thoroughfare is much as it used to be in days gone by.

Gartlet School

Gartlet private school for girls was originally founded by a Mrs Walker circa 1855 in Bushey, although with the steady increase in the number of pupils, it wasn't long before it was found necessary to relocate to larger premises in Fairfield House, which had been specially built for the school in Loates Lane. Following its transfer to Clarendon Road (above) in 1897, where it remained for over fifty years, the school moved to a lovely house called 'Baynards' in Nascot Wood Road under the guidance of the two joint heads, the Misses Howe and Hancock. With the addition of a gymnasium, library and a new block of form rooms, the school thrived, but eventually closed its doors for good in the late 1980s/early 1990s, the premises then being occupied by the award-winning Watford School of Music until they moved to their new home in Clarendon Muse at the Boys' Grammar School in 2008. The picture below shows one of the classrooms at the Clarendon Road site. Both Gartlet School premises in Clarendon Road and Nascot Wood Road have now been redeveloped into residential accommodation.

Gammons Lane Prefabs

Tucked away on a small triangular parcel of land in north Watford is the site of what was once the only development of prefabricated dwellings of the type shown, to be erected in the town during the immediate austere aftermath of the Second World War. Built as a temporary measure to help meet the acute housing shortage that existed at the time, the prefabs, with a planned life of only ten years, survived until the early 1960s when Hollytree House, a development of sheltered retirement accommodation, was constructed in 1968. The above picture shows the marked out plot, with the rear of the houses in Chilcott Road on the left and Courtlands Drive in the foreground. Gammons Lane is just out of camera shot on the right. The arrival on site of one of the units is depicted in the image below to await the delivery of further panels and final assembly. With two bedrooms, a bathroom with flushing toilet and fitted kitchen, the prefabs were to many occupants used to the pleasures of an outside lavatory and tin bath, the absolute epitome of 'luxury'.

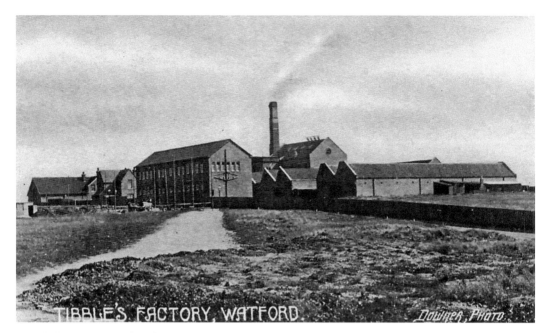

Dr Tibbles' Vi-Cocoa Chocolate Factory

It was in 1899 that a large chocolate factory, Dr Tibbles' Vi-Cocoa Company, opened in north Watford. Trading as the Watford Manufacturing Company, a range of cocoa products were produced including Vi-Cocoa, Coca tablets, Child's Restorer and Brain Feeder with advertisements claiming that these products offered many revitalising effects and health benefits. Up to a thousand workers were kept steadily employed in producing the various food delicacies and confections such as chocolates, cocoa, soups, jellies, blancmanges, custards and pudding powders 'right out in the country, away from all the contaminations of city air'. Factory tours were on offer where visitors could watch the various stages of food production in a scrupulously clean working environment.

The Great Fire at Dr Tibbles' Vi-Cocoa Factory

Watford's largest fire at that time was the conflagration that broke out in the early evening of Saturday 7 February 1903 at Dr Tibbles' Vi-Cocoa Factory attracting around 20,000 people from Watford and the surrounding area. The Watford brigade together with brigades from Sedgwick's Brewery, Bushey, Rickmansworth and Croxley were soon on the scene and despite sustaining extensive damage, much of the factory including the engine rooms, boiler sheds, carpenters' shop and a substantial amount of coal and timber were saved despite the low pressure of water available. Although the factory was closed for a substantial period of time, it was eventually rebuilt and during the First World War produced supplies for frontline troops. Despite expanding the premises during the immediate post-war years, the company went bankrupt in 1922, another sad casualty of 'lost Watford'. An Asda hypermarket now occupies the site.

Garston Crossroads

When compared to the earlier print above photographed circa 1914/15, today's view of this busy crossroads in Garston has changed out of all recognition. The building in the centre of the above picture is the Three Horseshoes public house, previously an old smithy and rebuilt around 1750, with the house on the left-hand side belonging to Sidney Waterton, a shopkeeper. The site of the old pub, which is depicted centrally in the bottom image, is now a flourishing Harvester restaurant.

Section 4
Watford Junction to Leavesden

The Golden Age of Steam

Every schoolboy's childhood dream in those halcyon pre-war days of the 1930s and the austere post-war period of the 1940s and '50s was to become an engine driver on famous locomotives such as the *Flying Scotsman* and *Mallard*. Failing that, there was always the innocent pastime of trainspotting, where the engine numbers of passing trains were eagerly crossed off in an Ian Allan ABC booklet, a publication that listed all of the relevant details, with the only outlay the cost of a platform ticket, a far cry from today's youngsters whose energies are devoted more to their Xboxes and iPads. The above picture shows an express train emerging from Watford Tunnel on its approach to the Junction. Originally, the route of the railway was planned to pass through the estates of the Earls of Essex and Clarendon, but due to their opposition, a new route that necessitated a cutting north of the Junction was put in place. The tunnel was 1 mile 170 yards long, 25 feet high and 24 feet wide and accommodated a two-track line. Ten workmen lost their lives during the excavation and construction in 1837.

Floods at Watford Junction

The presence of the photographer has certainly attracted an inquisitive crowd of onlookers as these youngsters, no doubt at the start of the school holidays, enjoy a summer paddle in the station forecourt after what was called the Great Storm of Monday 22 July 1907. The offices of the coal merchants Brentnall & Cleland Ltd can just be seen to the right of the picture, with the Temperance Refreshment Room next door but one also appearing to be experiencing the aftermath of the flood.

Junction Forecourt

A long-gone view of how the Junction forecourt looked in the early 1940s as passengers from the London trains queue for their buses home after buying a copy of the *Evening News* or *Evening Standard* giving accounts of all the latest War Bulletins. With the number of cars parked, it must only be a short while before petrol rationing started to take effect, and vehicles were only used for essential journeys. Hoarding advertisements proclaim the benefits of Guinness or Andrews Liver Salts, while a sign indicates the whereabouts of the 'American Red Cross Services Club'. How different the same vista looks today almost eighty years later.

Platforms 9, 10 and 11 at Watford Junction

These two lovely iconic photographs taken in 1943 show the platforms of 9, 10 and 11 at the top of the stairs from the access tunnel below. Bringing back nostalgic memories of a bygone age, an old steam engine can just be seen off centre in the top image, while an advertisement in the bottom photo from the Gaumont states that the latest film of the day, *The Youngest Profession*, starring Virginia Weidler and Edward Arnold, is now showing at the local cinema. A common sight on many station platforms in those days were the red cast-iron machines where a bar of Nestlé chocolate could be procured for the princely sum of 1*d*. Sadly, this special treat for numerous youngsters came to an end on 26 July 1942 when sweets and chocolate started to be rationed, with the machines remaining empty for the duration.

London Orphan School

Originally based in Clapton, the London Orphan School, or Asylum as it was originally called, was founded in 1813 by Andrew Reed as a charitable organisation 'to educate respectable fatherless children of either sex'. With concern for the poor health of the children following a serious outbreak of typhus, it was decided to construct a new institution on a beautiful site in Watford, deemed to be a healthier environment, and where there would be accommodation for 600 orphans. The asylum was opened in 1872 by Princess Mary of Cambridge, the Duchess of Teck. In 1915, it was renamed the London Orphan School and Reed's School in 1939. During the 1980s, following the granting of Grade II listed status in 1983, the buildings were converted into residential accommodation, as can be seen in the photograph below.

LONDON ORPHAN SCHOOL AND ROYAL BRITISH ORPHAN SCHOOL. WATFORD.
SENIOR BOYS' CLASSROOM.

London Orphan School

The two pictures depicted here show a carefully posed image of the senior boys' classroom, while the whole school (below) can be seen gathered for a group photograph, most of the youngsters looking as though they would rather be somewhere else.

Rose Tea Cottage

Originally called Rose Tea Cottage, this charming locally listed building in Watford Heath was formerly a tearoom with a lovely well-stocked garden to the rear containing ornate trelliswork and a pretty gazebo. The property was constructed in the mid-nineteenth century and may have been part of the Oxhey Grange estate's development of Watford Heath. An amusing anecdote at the time was that the owner of Oxhey Grange Developments, a devout Quaker, used the Rose Tea Gardens in an attempt to encourage the local workforce away from the nearby public houses. One can only speculate on how much success he had! Although still standing as Rose House, the tearoom and gardens are no more with the property now under private ownership.

Leavesden Asylum

Prior to 1867 psychiatric care in London was virtually non-existent. Patients were either left to roam the streets or were admitted to the workhouse or, at worst, the lunatic asylum. In the year of 1867, following the establishment of the Metropolitan Asylums Board, a 76-scre site was purchased at Leavesden near Watford, with the new building opening on 9 October 1870. During the following years, the emphasis changed from detention and segregation to prevention and treatment. This led to the gradual resettlement and integration of patients into the community, resulting in the termination of institutions such as Leavesden, which eventually closed in October 1995. The building has now been converted into private residential accommodation.

Leavesden Aerodrome

In 1940 during the early days of the Second World War, the Air Ministry decided to build an aircraft factory and airfield on land at Leavesden on the outskirts of Watford. It was here that a large number of de Havilland Mosquitoes and Handley Page Halifaxes were produced, subsequently playing a crucial role during the conflict. On the cessation of hostilities, the site eventually became a subsidiary of Rolls-Royce, building helicopter engines until final closure in 1992. The photographs show the site in the mid-1950s.

Leavesden Studios

In 1994, Eon Productions leased the unoccupied Leavesden site for the duration of their shoot on the latest James Bond film, with the old aircraft hangars well suited to conversion into film stages. Leavesden Studios as the site was now rebranded, produced a series of major feature films until the year 2000 when Heyday Films acquired the site on behalf of Warner Bros. Over the next ten years Leavesden Studios produced every one of the Harry Potter films until in November 2010 Warner Bros. completed its purchase of the site, which was now renamed Warner Bros Studios, Leavesden.

Almost twenty years after the complex was converted from aerodrome to film studios, the site now greatly enlarged was officially opened on 26 April 2013 by the Duke and Duchess of Cambridge. The two images show Leavesden Studios in 2011.

Leavesden Open Days

Three programme covers from
the Leavesden open days in 1974,
1980 and 1987.

Section 5
Cassio Hamlet to Hunton Bridge

Cassio Hamlet

The lovely wintry scene above shows Cassio Hamlet on Boxing Day 1906, an area that consisted of a small cluster of cottages just north of the Crossroads and two public houses, The Dog and The Horns. With this part of what is now Hempstead Road pedestrianised, it seems difficult to imagine that a hundred years ago, horse-drawn haywains used to trundle their heavy loads along this road to the weekly livestock market in the centre of Watford. Although the cottages and The Dog have long since gone, The Horns is still there, currently enjoying considerable popularity as a live music venue.

No longer a country lane, the thoroughfare is home to Watford Central Public Library, opened in 1928, the modern swimming pool complex of Watford Leisure Centre, Central, and West Herts College. Unaware of the photographer's presence, the small family group in the image below, possibly a nanny with her young charges, make their way towards the High Street, a lot of the charm of these pictures now lost to today's modern panorama.

Little Cassiobury

Little Cassiobury is believed to have been built in the late seventeenth century as a Dower House for Elizabeth Capell, the Countess of Essex. Born on 16 December 1636 at Petworth Manor, Sussex, she married Arthur Capell, 2nd Baron Capell of Hadham, later being created the 1st Earl of Essex by Charles II in 1661. On her husband's death by suicide in the Tower of London in 1683, her son Algernon succeeded to the title becoming the 2nd Earl of Essex, with Elizabeth taking up residence at Little Cassiobury until her death in 1718. Today, as a Grade II listed building and after lying vacant for a number of years, the property has fallen into a state of disrepair. With its past splendour now lost in the mists of time, Little Cassiobury as a building of considerable historical significance has had a survey commissioned to suggest sustainable options for its future.

GROVE MILL LANE WATFORD

Grove Mill

The tranquil setting above was Grove Mill, built in 1875 to produce flour for The Grove estate, with the miller and his mill hands living in the adjoining house and cottages. The small wooden structure attached to the top level of the mill was known as a lucum, or sack hoist, where the newly delivered bags of corn were lifted by chain from the cart below. Once the flour had been ground, the reverse process would take place with the sacks being lowered onto the waiting transport for delivery to the estate. Opposite the mill is the Dower House, built by the Earl of Clarendon for his mother, the dowager, Countess of Clarendon. Following a long period of disuse when the old mill fell into a state of disrepair, it eventually underwent a complete renovation and was tastefully converted into flats during the early 1970s. The picture below is looking in the opposite direction to the mill up Grove Mill Lane.

Grove Mill Lane, Watford.

A Royal Visitor to Watford

Watford residents were out in force on Saturday 17 July 1909 to welcome the arrival of Edward VII, whose small cavalcade of vehicles is seen entering the main entrance to The Grove estate. Having just motored up from Sandown Races, His Majesty was making a short 'Saturday to Monday' visit, as the weekend was then called, to his friend the Earl of Clarendon. What is most noticeable from this historic image, when compared to modern-day safeguards, is the complete lack of security, as the loyal crowds press forward to cheer and wave their sovereign into The Grove.

H.M. THE KING'S VISIT TO THE 'GROVE' WATFORD, JULY 17 09. ENTERING THE GATES.   DOWNER. PHOTO

The Grove

This imposing mansion, The Grove, set in the beautiful Hertfordshire countryside was once the ancestral home of the Earls of Clarendon. It was here that many fashionable weekend parties were held, one of the most important guests being Edward VII who made a short visit to The Grove on Saturday 17 July 1909, attending Divine Service at St Mary's Church the following day. However, in 1922, the Clarendon family's long association with The Grove ended when the estate was sold by the 6th Earl, George Herbert Hyde Villiers, who had decided to move to Hampstead in London. For a while, a high-class girls' school occupied the premises until, at the outbreak of the Second World War, the London, Midland & Scottish Railway (LMS) acquired The Grove for the duration, moving their headquarters from London. Following the cessation of hostilities in 1945 and several changes of occupancy over the years, The Grove now enjoys a new resurgence as a prestigious hotel, spa and golf course.

Hunton Bridge Filling Station

This lovely old photo circa mid-1920s shows the Hunton Bridge Filling Station, just a short distance from The Grove, at a time when the pace of life was more tranquil and traffic-free than it is today, and the price of petrol was only around 1s 5d a gallon. The car is a Citroen C2, known in France as the Trefle (Cloverleaf), also commonly known as a 5CV, and was produced between 1922 and 1926. It may well have been one of the original models to be produced at Citroen's first overseas factory in Slough. It is interesting to see that the attendant, no doubt justifiably proud, is using one of the new Fry Guaranteed Visible Measure Petrol Pumps where the amount of fuel selected filled a transparent glass bowl. The motorist could then check to see that the number of gallons being dispensed and the particular grade, denoted by the colour of the petrol, was what had been requested. Over ninety years later, petrol is still dispensed on the same site albeit on a self-service basis, while a range of snacks and other goods can be purchased from the modern service station and convenience shop. With the old filling station lost forever, these nostalgic snapshots conjure up the way things were in the early days of motoring.

Hunton Bridge Mill

This large, rural watermill at Hunton Bridge on what was once called the Grand Junction Canal was, in 1544, owned by Sir Richard Lee, and was originally constructed to harness the power of the River Gade. For nearly thirty years between 1826 and 1855 the miller was one John Carpenter, with the Puttnams running two mills in the 1920s – Hunton Bridge and Grove Mill. During the Second World War, Hunton Bridge Mill was used as a small munitions factory, but after the cessation of hostilities, it was demolished, probably due to road improvements on a blind bend in Old Mill Road. Although in an inoperative state, the waterwheel still survives. With a diameter of approximately 10 feet and a width of 13 feet, this overshot wheel of five bays has an estimated total of 200 buckets. All that remains today is the mill stream from the canal, the waterwheel and an impressive 200-year-old mill house.

Section 6

Rickmansworth Road and West Watford

Peace Memorial Hospital

Opened in 1925 by the Princess Royal at a cost of £90,000, the Peace Memorial Hospital was built to replace the old Cottage Hospital in Vicarage Road, although by the late 1930s even this new accommodation was found to be inadequate to meet the needs of a fast-expanding area. In response to an appeal, a further £70,000 was raised by generous public subscription to provide much needed extensions. In July 1928, a splendid statue of three figures sculptured by Mary Pownall Bromet and dedicated 'To the Fallen', 'Victory' and 'To the Wounded' was unveiled by the Earl of Clarendon. Known as *The Spirit of War*, the statue is now situated by the Town Hall. With the expansion of the West Herts Hospital in Vicarage Road, the Rickmansworth Road site eventually closed, and although much of the old hospital infrastructure has now disappeared, the original building remains as the Watford Peace Hospice.

PEACE MEMORIAL HOSPITAL, WATFORD.   H.6902.

Watford West Station

Watford West station in Tolpits Lane as it used to look, and as it appeared until comparatively recently – overgrown with undergrowth and flora. Only the concrete platform remains, together with the rusting tracks where once steam trains travelled. The station was opened in 1912 as part of the Croxley Green branch line, which ran from Croxley Green to Watford Junction, via Watford West, Watford Stadium and Watford High Street. The station was temporarily shut in 1996 together with the remainder of the line, but was eventually closed permanently in 2001. Discussions had taken place regarding the proposed Croxley Rail Link and the possible reopening of the old branch line, with Watford West enjoying a new revival, but this was not to be. Although vegetation started to be cleared in 2013, work was subsequently stopped, with the Metropolitan line extension effectively abandoned.

Vicarage Road Cemetery

Two images of Vicarage Road in the early 1900s with the cemetery, which was opened in 1858, depicted in the top picture. Originally, the small chapel above only served the Anglican denomination, but following the demolition of the Nonconformist mortuary chapel that was situated just out of camera shot, the remaining chapel now serves all Christian denominations, although today is rarely used. The bottom picture taken from Vicarage Road shows a lovely old building that was once the lodge to the cemetery and was used as offices for Watford Burial Board. Following demolition in 1959 – another part of lost Watford – a new lodge was built, which just did not portray any of the characteristics of the original.

Shrodells

Constructed in 1838 as the Union Workhouse, this rather grim-looking early Victorian building in Vicarage Road with its prison-like appearance used to serve the basic needs of the poor within the parish, where they could obtain one good meal a day and a bed for the night. In return, adults and young children were hired out to households and local factory owners to undertake a range of menial tasks, very often for long and arduous hours. In 1930, the name 'Shrodells' (meaning 'shrubberies') was adopted when the Board of Guardians was replaced by the Watford Guardians Committee. The old Grade II listed institution now forms part of Watford General Hospital and is currently used for administrative purposes.

Scammell's

This interesting photograph was taken at Scammell Lorries in Tolpits Lane, probably just after the outbreak of the Second World War. A lot of the men gathered are wearing helmets with the letters 'AFS' emblazoned on the front. This indicates that they were part of the Auxiliary Fire Service, formed from volunteers prior to September 1939 to assist the regular fire brigades. The name was changed in August 1941 to the National Fire Service when the regulars and the AFS merged for the duration. Also pictured are members of the Civil Defence Corps. During hostilities, Scammell's made an immense contribution to the war effort by building large numbers of heavy recovery vehicles, Pioneer tank transporters as well as autocoupling conversions and fire pumps, etc. The bottom picture shows a Scammell's Fire Fighting demonstration on 17 May 1939. Sadly, in February 1987, the news was announced that the factory was to close with the final curtain coming down on one of Britain's greatest commercial institutions in July 1988. The site was subsequently redeveloped into residential housing.

The Watford and District Isolation Hospital

In 1893, an Act was passed relating to the provision of isolation hospitals in order to cater for the needs and care of those unfortunate enough to have contracted one of many infectious diseases. In Watford, suitable land in Tolpits Lane was donated by the Earl of Essex for the proposed site of the new Watford Isolation Hospital. The hospital took seventeen months to complete at a cost of just over £12,000, with the opening ceremony taking place on 24 March 1896 and performed by the Countess of Essex. With the creation of the National Health Service in 1948, the hospital was renamed the Holywell Hospital and became part of the NHS, but in 1982 the hospital finally closed with all services transferred to Watford General Hospital. It was demolished in 1985. Today the site has been redeveloped for housing. The picture below shows a ward Christmas party put on by the nursing staff to bring at least a little seasonal cheer into the young patients' lives.

Sun Printers

During the last 100 years, Watford was known worldwide as a centre for high-class commercial printing. It was in 1906 that a large print works was established in Whippendell Road, west Watford, called the Sun Engraving Company, employing over a thousand people. In 1945, following the end of the Second World War, Sun Engraving was sold to Hazell, Watson and Viney of Aylesbury who then formed the Hazell Sun Group as a holding company for its various production outlets. The Whippendell Road site was then renamed Sun Printers, entering into a period of sustained expansion, but by the early 1980s, with the company now in financial difficulties, Sun Print Works finally closed. The infrastructure was demolished in 2000, following which the site was redeveloped into a hotel, shops, housing and industrial units.

The Clock Tower

The top image shows the iconic Clock Tower, originally constructed in 1934 for the Sun Engraving Company as a water-pumping station over an artesian well, thus enabling the company to overcome the existing problems of a fluctuating water supply, which tended to occur in times of low rainfall. The water was pumped to the boiler house and onwards to the rotary gravure presses in order to steam-dry the ink. Although Sun Printers is no more, the Clock Tower remains, despite now looking somewhat the worse for wear due to vandalism and theft, and without its dials. It is now scheduled for renovation. The lovely picture below depicts a pen and ink drawing of the tower.

Section 7
Along the Canal to Cassiobury

The Canal

Originally known as the Grand Junction Canal, part of the waterway system connecting London and Birmingham, the company was bought by the Regent's Canal in 1927 before amalgamating with several other companies to form the Grand Union Canal in 1929. As dawn breaks in the above image, two fully laden working narrowboats glide into the early mist of a sunny autumn morning, bound no doubt for one of the canalside industries based further up the cut. Featured below in this charming, tranquil setting at Ironbridge Lock No. 77 in the beautiful Cassiobury Park, two narrowboats can be seen continuing their journey, while outside the lock-keeper's cottage, now long-since gone, a tow horse is obviously enjoying his nosebag of feed and a well-earned rest.

Canal Life.

CANAL LOCKS WATFORD

The Emergence of Leisure Craft

Depicted in a lovely picture postcard dated 16 August 1907, two more working narrowboats are waiting to exit Lock No. 77, but the 'writing was already on the wall' as gradually this hard way of life started to disappear, as other and faster modes of transport took over as the canal system slowly went into decline. With the nostalgic passing of the old freight-carrying narrowboats that hauled coal and other commodities, came the emergence of leisure craft – boats that were bought to live on, or hired for weekends, or as in the case of the image below, used as a passenger-carrying service for short trips up the canal. Bryan Nicoll, a keen narrowboat enthusiast, purchased *Arcturus* in December 1958 and following repairs and conversion started his service, eventually running trips from Ironbridge Lock No. 77 in Cassiobury Park from 1966 until October 1999, when sadly both owner and boat retired.

The Mill, Cassiobury Park, Watford 343|7

The Old Mill

Hidden among the trees next to the weir at the bottom of Cassiobury Park is the site of the Old Mill, once used to grind corn and later utilised for the pumping of water to Cassiobury House. Following the demolition of the mansion in 1927, the mill fell into a state of disrepair and in 1956 was eventually knocked down and removed, although after more than sixty years there are still signs of this historic structure to be seen. Some of the foundations are plainly visible from the opposite riverbank, while the brick arches over the mill stream, as seen below, are even now very much in evidence – a small remnant of a bygone age.

Grove Mill, Watford.

The Old Mill and Weir

This lovely picture of the weir and the Old Mill in its heyday located next to what was then the Grand Junction Canal, now the Grand Union. A hot, sultry summer's day shows a group of happy youngsters below splashing in the cool water of the weir – no doubt deemed to be a health and safety hazard nowadays.

The River Gade

These two coloured images, both captured in the late 1960s/early 1970s, show the River Gade meandering through the lower part of Cassiobury Park. The top picture shows the popular paddling pool in the background constructed in 1933, where many a happy hour was spent by children in their summer holidays enjoying this watery oasis or sailing a toy yacht. A few boys can be seen angling in the bottom photo where if you were very lucky you might just catch a roach, which could weigh in at a respectable 2 lb, but more than likely it was a small minnow that took the bait at the end of the hook.

The River Gade in Cassiobury Park, Watford.   ET.371

Conker Time!

The young lads above could be trying to catch the falling leaves, or, more probably, attempting to gather the spiky horse chestnuts for the time-honoured annual tradition of playing conkers. Today, with numerous gadgetry such as iPhones, iPads and PlayStations to occupy their time, the game would appear to be in a state of decline.

A New Paddling Pool

In the early 1980s, the paddling pool was filled in and grassed over when a modern play area and a cluster of new pools with fountains replaced the outdated facilities, ensuring that the comprehensive amenities on offer would be as popular as ever to the thousands of visitors from far and wide who come to the lovely award-winning park each year. However, after over thirty years, the amenities were starting to look a little rundown and in considerable need of a major facelift. This resulted in a multimillion-pound project commencing in 2011, with money allocated by the Heritage Lottery Fund and the Big Lottery Fund. On 1 July 2017, a new state-of-the-art water play park with splash pads, water jets and fountains, together with two new paddling pools was opened, with a hub containing a kiosk, café, changing rooms and toilets, and community and exhibition space.

The Bandstand

Each Sunday throughout the summer months, the rousing marches of John Philip Sousa and other well-known composers could be heard echoing around Cassiobury Park as a military band played to a captive audience from the fine, elegant-looking bandstand originally built in 1912 and situated not far from the Pavilion Tearooms. For 3*d*, the price of a deckchair, one could sit and relax, listening to the music and watching the world go by. This quintessentially English pastime continued until the late 1930s when, with the outbreak of the Second World War, the bandstand fell into disuse. It was eventually dismantled, and after several years was re-erected in the precinct opposite the Town Hall next to the Central Library in 1975. Today, this lovely old bandstand has been completely renovated and returned to its rightful place at the top of Cassiobury Park, opening on Sunday 4 September 2016.

Cassiobury Park. Watford.

The Pavilion Tearooms

Postmarked 7 November 1929, this Real Photo picture postcard shows a view of the Cassiobury Park fountain with the Pavilion Tearooms in the background. Both features were constructed circa 1925, and although the fountain was removed sometime after the mid-1960s, the tearooms remain. Today, after a complete refurbishment paid for by the two Lottery Funds, and a new name, the ever-popular Cha Café run by Mandy, ably assisted by Brian and all the team, provides an invaluable service with a comprehensive menu in a friendly atmosphere throughout the year to all who visit the lovely park. The drinking fountain, which has been fully restored, has now been returned to its original location.

Cassiobury House

Pictured in the early part of the twentieth century, it is difficult to imagine that this magnificent mansion, Cassiobury House, seat of the Earls of Essex, would eventually be razed to the ground. Following the death in 1916 of George Devereux de Vere Capell, the 7th Earl, his wife Adele, the countess dowager of Essex, sold the estate in 1922 for building development; however, with no purchaser for the house, it was left empty and derelict for a further five years until its demolition in 1927, with a sale of building materials taking place on site during Wednesday 9 November 1927. The ornate Grinling Gibbons main staircase of Cassiobury House, seen in the image below, was carefully removed and is now in the Metropolitan Museum of Art in New York – the end of an era.

Park Gates

Friday 24 July 1970 was indeed a black day for Watfordians when the demolition men started to reduce a piece of Watford's heritage to rubble. The historic, castellated, Tudor-style lodge gates giving access from Rickmansworth Road to the lovely Cassiobury Park, were originally built as the entrance to the long driveway leading to Cassiobury House, but due to an essential road-widening scheme their fate was sealed and they had to go. Where the gates once stood at the entrance to Cassiobury, the jewel in Watford's crown, now proudly flutters a Green Flag from its pole. This prestigious award, the twelfth for Watford, is only granted to those parks that have met a set of key criteria, with the town now having more Green Flag awards than any other district in Hertfordshire.

Park Gates

Two beautiful illustrations of the long-gone park gates are shown here, with a snowy scene above taken from Rickmansworth Road, little more than a lane in those days, in the early years of the twentieth century. And below is a view of the colourful flower beds, located just inside the gates. This photograph was captured sometime during the early to mid-1960s.

Section 8
Entertainment and Leisure

THE WATFORD FOOTBALL TEAM, 1907-8.

J. Goodall. A. Hitch. C. Aston. W. Biggar. H. B. Watkins, Esq. H. W. Higgins. A. Betts. J. Richardson. J. Upton
(Manager). (Vice-Chairman). (Trainer).
H. O. Badger. J. Reynolds. W. Eames. F. C. Robins, Esq. R. A. Thorpe, Esq. J. Foster. G. M. Furr. A. Soar.
(Secretary). (Chairman).
C. Fyfe. J. Wright. W. Law.

Watford Football Club

These two iconic photographs taken during the season of 1907–08 show Watford Football Club at their old home ground in Cassio Road where they were based between 1898 and 1922. Following their election to the Football League in 1920, their first League match was a 2-0 defeat by Queens Park Rangers on 4 September 1920. Before moving to their new ground at Vicarage Road, their last League game was held on 29 April 1922 where they beat Gillingham 1-0 in front of 5,000 spectators. The image below shows the match between Watford and Bristol Rovers on 5 October 1907 and what looks like a heading contest in front of the Bristol goal. Watford lost to Bristol 1-2. Cassio Road is now the West Herts Sports Ground, and remains as a sports venue.

WATFORD 1, BRISTOL ROVERS 2, OCT 5TH 1907. A HEADING CONTEST IN FRONT OF BRISTOL GOAL.

Herts Bowling Club

On 27 August 1911, an inaugural meeting was held in Bucks Restaurant, High Street, Watford, to form a bowls club, with the name being adopted as the Herts Bowling Club. The President, Mr J. F. Watkins, opened the new green in Mildred Avenue on Wednesday 1 May 1912. The clubhouse is depicted to the left of the above image, with St Michael and all Angels' Church featured on the right. When a fine new and larger church was constructed, the consecration taking place on 19 January 1913, the old church was subsequently used as St Michael's Hall. The picture below shows the bowls club prior to 1915, eventually moving its location to Bellmount Wood Avenue on the Cassiobury estate on 26 September 1988. The Mildred Avenue site has now been developed into tasteful residential accommodation aptly called Bowling Court.

The River Colne Bathing Lido

It was here in the shadow of the Five Arches railway viaduct over the River Colne (above) that an open-air public bathing place was cordoned off to form a large square-shaped lido during the summer of 1906. Around this area were a number of wooden changing cubicles and a spectators' viewing gallery. Certain hours were set aside for ladies and the season extended from around the middle of April to the middle of October. The Watford Amateur Swimming Club did much to promote the success of the bathing place and the encouragement of swimming, holding its annual gala there, which was always well attended. However, conditions were most unhygienic when compared to modern standards. Following the discovery of sewage in 1936, a decision was made by Watford Council for the lido to be closed, no doubt an unpopular ruling for many, despite the new indoor swimming pool that had opened in Hempstead Road three years earlier.

Watford Central Swimming Baths

Two images of the River Colne Lido are shown above including the opening ceremony on 9 June 1906. As can be seen, this was a popular venue for many years until due to the somewhat unhygienic conditions that existed when compared with modern standards, a decision was made to close the lido, especially as the new Central Swimming Baths in Hempstead Road (below) had opened three years earlier in 1933. With the move to Hempstead Road, swimmers were not only able to enjoy undercover bathing all year round in what was believed to have been the world's first electrically heated pool, but also included amenities such as a spring board, high diving board and a water chute, although these were eventually removed as they were deemed to be a safety hazard. After more than seventy years of swimming at Watford Central, the baths eventually closed for major redevelopment in December 2006, reopening again twenty months later in August 2008 with a new pool under the changed name of Watford Leisure Centre, Central.

The Palace Theatre

Situated a few yards from the High Street in Clarendon Road is arguably one of the country's finest theatres – the Watford Palace. This lovely Edwardian structure opened on Monday 14 December 1908 with a *High Class Vaudeville Company* under the direction of T. M. Sylvester. When other provincial theatres have closed, the Palace has thrived for over a hundred years, providing high-class and varied entertainment to the local community and beyond. The actors and actresses who have trodden the boards are a who's who of show business, sadly no longer with us, ranging from celebrities such as George Robey, Gracie Fields ('Our Gracie') and Jack Hylton and his Band to local boy, the comedian Terry Scott and Anthony Booth, the father of Cherie Blair, wife of the former prime minister, to name but a few. This postcard from the late 1950s also shows John Collier 'the window to watch' men's outfitters, previously the Fifty Shilling Tailors, on the corner site now occupied by a branch of the Halifax Building Society. Depicted below is an early photograph of The Palace and the inset is a programme from 1917.

The Carlton Cinema

Adjacent to the theatre is the building that was to become the Carlton Cinema. Originally called The Super, this was a conversion of a roller-skating rink. Although it did not provide the ideal shape for a cinema auditorium, everything was done to achieve the best possible conditions, including a seating capacity of 1,228. During late 1930, the Super changed its name to the Carlton and, following extensive alterations, continued playing to audiences until its closure on Saturday 12 July 1980, with its final film performance of *Zombies – Dawn of the Dead*. The Carlton was demolished in 1982, with the site now occupied, in part, by an extension of the Palace Theatre.

62. CENTRAL HALL PICTURE HOUSE.

Central Hall Picture House

Opening on Wednesday 17 December 1913, the Central Hall Picture House in King Street (Watford's first large cinema, with a seating capacity of just over 1,000) included in the audience the Earl of Clarendon and Lord and Lady Hyde, who watched the comedy film *A Regiment for Two* together with several other general interest films. All takings that evening were donated to charity. The cinema opened daily from 2.30 p.m. except Sundays, with seating prices ranging from 3*d* to 1*s* depending on whether the patron requested a stalls seat or balcony seat. With name changes taking place on 30 September 1929 to the Regal and on 9 July 1956 to the Essoldo, the cinema eventually decided to opt for the more lucrative takings from bingo. Today, although the art deco façade remains, the building has now been converted into residential accommodation.

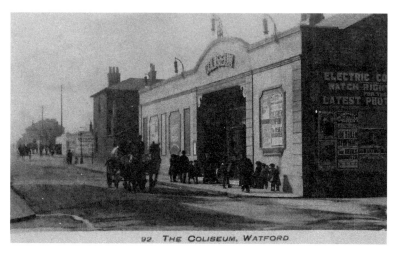

92. THE COLISEUM, WATFORD

The Electric Coliseum Cinema

This 650-seat cinema in St Albans Road tended to cater for the entertainment needs of the people living mostly in terraced housing in north Watford. It opened on 1 October 1912 with its first feature film *The Black Panther* accompanied by a pianist on an Ascherberg piano. The cinema was especially popular with soldiers during the early days of the First World War who had been billeted in the area before their inevitable postings to the horrors of northern France. On 21 December 1936, the cinema was renamed the Plaza following the other Plaza cinema on The Parade in the High Street being acquired by the Odeon circuit, thus becoming the Odeon. These were the golden days of the cinema with their art deco façades and garish neon lighting, when patrons could forget the realities of everyday life watching the latest feature films in the smoky atmosphere of the auditorium. The final programme before closure on Saturday 31 July 1954 was *Bomba and the Jungle Girl* and *Wild Stallion*. Demolition took place in 1957 with the site now occupied by Tyre City.

Mʳ WILLOW'S "CITY OF CARDIFF". THE FIRST AIR-SHIP SEEN IN WATFORD. MARCH 5ᵗʰ 1911

City of Cardiff at Watford .

During a blustery week in early March 1911, the *City of Cardiff* airship, piloted by the pioneer Welsh aviator and airship builder Mr E. T. Willows, was reported to have been a great centre of attraction on its arrival in Watford, where it had been housed in a temporary hangar on a field just off Bushey Hall Road. Shortly after 5 p.m. on Sunday 5 March, the enthralled crowd of spectators were treated to the exciting spectacle of the airship taking off, when it proceeded to make a wide circle over the town for around thirty minutes.

THE £10,000 AEROPLANE FLIGHT FROM LONDON TO MANCHESTER
M. PAULHAN, THE WINNER, PASSING OVER WATFORD, APRIL 27TH 1910

Downer, Photo.

Aeroplane Race Over Watford

Excited crowds turned out to see the London to Manchester aeroplane race passing over Watford on 27 April 1910, the first time that a flying machine had been seen in the area. The prize of £10,000 was offered by the *Daily Mail* to the first pilot to make the flight within twenty-four hours. The winner was French aviator Louis Paulhan, covering the distance of 195 miles in a time of twelve hours, thus beating the British contender, Claude Grahame-White.

Acknowledgements

I am extremely grateful to the following for their kind assistance in not only loaning rare and iconic picture postcards for scanning purposes, but also for providing superb photographic archive material and helpful and constructive advice and comments, and for giving me the benefit of their specialised local history knowledge, all greatly appreciated:

Lynda Bullock, West Watford History Group
Sue Ettridge, West Watford History Group
Mandy and Brian Evans, The Cha Café
Mary Forsyth, Watford Museum
Pat Greville, The Greville Collection
Herts Bowling Club
David Huggins, Avenue Collectables
John Kirkham
Roger Middleton, Curator, Watford Fire Museum
Cynthia and John Morgan
Simon Murphy, Curator, London Transport Museum
Bryan Nicoll
Richard Riding
David Spain
Watford Central Library
Watford Museum

Special thanks are extended to my wife Betty for her constant support, encouragement and invaluable input, to my son Mark for his continuous IT support, and to my publisher for their kind assistance in producing this book.

Every endeavour has been made to contact all copyright holders and any errors that have occurred are inadvertent. Anyone who for any reason has not been contacted is invited to write to the publisher so that a full acknowledgement may be made in any subsequent edition of this book.